Alice Merrill Horne
1868-1948

WRITTEN BY
Lola Beatlebrox

ILLUSTRATED BY
Anita Crane

"If this were my last hour and if it were within my power to bestow on my people
a priceless legacy, I would write it in these three words: "Cherish Your Artists."

–Alice Merrill Horne

Alice Merrill Horne was born in a log cabin in Fillmore, Utah. Alice was a little child when she went to live with her grandmother, Bathsheba Smith. Her grandfather had died and her grandmother was very lonely. Alice traveled all the way from Fillmore to her grandmother's house in Salt Lake City.

Her grandmother's house was full of treasures – at least it seemed so to Alice. Her grandfather had traveled to many faraway places in the world. There were two Chinese tea boxes filled with photographs. Since photographs were fairly new in 1876, these pictures were very precious. Alice was allowed to look at them ever so carefully, which she did at least twice a day.

1

Alice also loved the boxes filled with marble stones from Greek temples, silk bandanas from Cairo and Palestine, and a fez cap worn by men in Turkey. "Each day was as if I had rubbed a ring and a genie came to satisfy my wish," said Alice, who loved most of all to read and learn about many new and wonderful things.

When Alice was fourteen years old, she went to school at the University of Deseret. She started a Shakespeare Society with her friends, who loved to wear costumes and read the plays of William Shakespeare out loud. One of the young men in her Shakespeare club was George Horne. Alice and George fell in love and married in 1890.

In 1893, Alice and George traveled by train to the World's Fair in Chicago. They also visited art museums in Boston, New York and Washington, D.C. This trip made a deep impression on Alice. She wanted everyone in Utah to be able to enjoy beautiful art, just as she had.

Alice had an idea – use some of Utah's tax money to buy beautiful paintings by Utah artists and hang the paintings in places where people could see them. To convince lawmakers to vote for her idea, Alice became a lawmaker herself. She was elected to the Utah State Legislature in 1898. Alice worked very hard to make other lawmakers pay attention to her idea. She even gave them flowers.

Alice's "Art Bill" passed into law in 1899. The new law created the Utah Art Institute and established the first state arts council in the nation. Many beautiful paintings were purchased. Alice wanted to show the paintings all over Utah but she hadn't learned how to drive. Her son Albert drove instead. He was only eleven years old. Alice had the car's pedals fitted with blocks of wood and off they went.

Alice also opened two art galleries where Utah artists could sell their paintings – one in the historic ZCMI tea room, the other in the Oak Room of the Newhouse Hotel. She was very concerned that people in Utah should help artists make a living by buying their artwork. "Artists cannot paint if they cannot eat," Alice said.

In 1932, Alice held art shows in 40 schools so the children could learn about the pictures. At West Junior High and Washington Elementary, each student paid 10 cents toward the purchase of an oil painting for the school. Because of Alice, many schools in Utah now have fine art collections.

Alice Merrill Horne had many, many friends. She was kind and considerate to everyone. When she believed something should be done, she was very determined. She asked her friends to support her projects and help solve problems. She was a champion of artists, the founder of the Utah Arts Council, and one of the most remarkable women that ever lived in Utah.

"If art reigns in the home, there will grow out of it beautiful parks, streets, thoroughfares and cities." *–Alice Merrill Horne*

ABOUT THE BOOK

The Utah Arts Council, the Utah State Legislature, the Western States Arts Federation, and the National Endowment for the Arts have supported *Early Utah Masterpieces: Alice Art Collection*, Utah's 2007 *American Masterpieces* project. *American Masterpieces: Three Centuries of Artistic Genius*, a special initiative of the National Endowment for the Arts, presents to Americans the best of their artistic and cultural legacy, reaching large and small communities in all fifty states.

Early Utah Masterpieces celebrates the extraordinary and rich historical significance of early Utah visual artists. The *Early Utah Masterpieces* traveling exhibit is providing constituents and visitors throughout the state of Utah an opportunity to view first hand and learn about the early history of painting in Utah. This companion children's booklet about the life of Alice Merrill Horne tells the story of a woman's passion for promoting and preserving Utah's artistic heritage.

ABOUT THE AUTHOR

Lola Beatlebrox is an author and a curriculum developer for nonprofit organizations. After 20 years in corporate education, teaching children is tremendously gratifying because, she says, "They pay attention." Ms. Beatlebrox has developed curriculum plans for the Park City Historical Society & Museum, Thanksgiving Point Institute and Recycle Utah. She is writing a Children's History of Summit County. She lives with her husband, two dogs, three cats and three llamas in Peoa, Utah.

ABOUT THE ILLUSTRATOR

Anita "Neets" Crane is an artist, photographer and writer. She has more than a dozen published books in the children's craft and art genres including *Victorian Chic* and *Teddy Bear Magic*. *Victorian Chic* features historic Park City homes and was second in nationwide sales for the *Country Home & Gardens* greeting cards. She lives with her fluffy-not-fat cat Ruby and her husband, Bruce, in Park City, Utah.

Design and layout by Laura Ann Ellingson

The Utah Arts Council is part of the Division of Arts and Museums housed within the Utah Department of Community and Culture. For information and resources, please visit arts.utah.gov.

Note: Every reasonable effort has been made to obtain proper permissions and to provide appropriate credit in this booklet. However, where sufficient supporting information is not available, the credit acknowledgment is limited to identification of the collections and or contributors involved.

First Edition
ISBN 0-9762675-3-5
UAC20070718

Utah Arts Council
617 East South Temple
Salt Lake City, Utah 84102